East India Company

The debate at the general quarterly court held at the East India

house

on Wednesday, June 19, 1799

East India Company

The debate at the general quarterly court held at the East India house
on Wednesday, June 19, 1799

ISBN/EAN: 9783743383753

Manufactured in Europe, USA, Canada, Australia, Japa

Cover: Foto ©Suzi / pixelio.de

Manufactured and distributed by brebook publishing software
(www.brebook.com)

East India Company

The debate at the general quarterly court held at the East India house

THE
DEBATE

AT THE

GENERAL QUARTERLY COURT

HELD AT

THE EAST INDIA HOUSE,

ON

WEDNESDAY, JUNE 19, 1799,

TO TAKE INTO CONSIDERATION THE PAPERS RESPECTING

ILLICIT TRADE,

Which were printed in confequence of a Refolution of the GENERAL COURT on the 20th of March laft; and other purpofes, for which the Court was made Special.

At which Court a Motion was made, and after Debate carried *unanimoufly* as follows :

RESOLVED, That it does not appear to the fatisfaction of this Court, from the Papers printed for their confideration, that it was neceffary to include the name of David Scott, fenior, in any Bill of Difcovery; but as the Court of Directors have thought proper, at the requeft of Mr. Scott himfelf (although not confiftent with the Refolution of the laft General Court), to prepare a Bill including his name, and to fubmit the fame to his Majefty's Attorney General, this Court do acquiefce therein: but they think it incumbent upon them at the fame time to declare, that they do not fee from thefe papers the fmalleft reafon to fufpect Mr. Scott of having betrayed any confidential knowledge which he poffeffed as a Member of the Secret Committee, or any part of his duty as a Director of this Company, or of having any perfonal knowledge of the Ship Helfingoer, or of tranfactions relative to the Trade of the Houfe of David Scott and Company, and that they entirely concur with the Court of Directors in acquitting him of all perfonal imputation.

———●·ΙΙ·●———

REPORTED

BY WILLIAM WOODFALL.

1799.

LONDON:

PRINTED FOR THE REPORTER,

(BY T. GILLET, CROWN-COURT, FLEET-STREET,)

AND SOLD BY J. DEBRETT, PICCADILLY; BYFIELD AND HAWKESWORTH, CHARING-CROSS; T. WOODFALL, NO. 101, DRURY-LANE; AND MURRAY AND HIGHLEY, FLEET-STREET;

Of whom may be had,

Mr. Woodfall's Reports of Eaft India Houfe Debates within the laft five years.

[Price Two Shillings.]

EAST INDIA HOUSE.

QUARTERLY GENERAL COURT.

WEDNESDAY, JUNE 19, 1799.

THE proceedings of the laſt General Court, recommending the conſideration of Lord Nelſon's ſervices to the Court of Directors, and alſo, recommending the not including Mr. David Scott, ſenior's name in a Bill of Diſcovery, were read by the Clerk.

The CHAIRMAN informed the Court, that this being a Quarterly General Court, it was neceſſary to declare the dividend on the Company's ſtock, from the 5th of January laſt to the 5th of July next, he therefore moved, that the reſolution of the Court of Directors that the ſame ſhould be five and a quarter *per cent.* be confirmed; which was unanimouſly agreed to.

The CHAIRMAN then ſtated, that by the third Chapter of the ſeventh Section of the By Laws, a Committee of By Laws was to be annually choſen at this time, he ſhould therefore deſire that the names of thoſe Gentlemen who had ſerved laſt year ſhould be read, and it would be neceſſary that they ſhould be put in nomination ſeparately. He was ſorry to inform them, that one of the committee (Mr. Blackburn) was dead, and it would be neceſſary to fill up the vacancy.

The ſix following Gentlemen, being the former members of the Committee, were then ſeparately named and re-elected, viz :

B   John

John Cornwall, Efq.   Henry Strachey, Efq.
Robert Hunter, Efq.   Samuel Wegg, Efq. and
Robert Holford, Efq.   George Wilton, Efq.
And in the room of Mr. Blackburn, William Drew, Efq.

The CHAIRMAN alfo informed the Court, that by the 11th Sect. of the third Chapter of the By-Laws, it was neceffary that the whole of the By-Laws fhould be read at the prefent Quarterly Court. He fhould therefore move, *pro forma*, that they fhould be read in the abftract; which being done, the Chairman faid, he had now to communicate to the Court the unanimous refolution of the Court of Directors conveying the thanks of the Company to Lord Nelfon, and that in confequence of the Court of Proprietors having referred it to their Executive Body to confider of a fuitable reward for thofe fervices, they had taken the fame into their confideration and had come to an unanimous refolution which he begged might be read. The Clerk then read the following refolution :

At a COURT *of* DIRECTORS, *held* 24th *April,* 1799.

Refolved Unanimoufly, That the thanks of this Court be given to the Right Honourable Rear Admiral Lord NELSON, for the very great and important fervices he has rendered to the Eaft India Company, by the ever-memorable victory obtained over the French fleet, near the Mouth of the Nile, on the 1ft, 2d, and 3d of Auguft, 1798.

Refolved Unanimoufly, That in further teftimony of the high fenfe this Court entertain of the very great and important benefits arifing to the Eaft India Company from his Lordfhip's magnanimous conduct on that glorious occafion, this Court requeft his Lordfhip's acceptance of the fum of Ten Thoufand Pounds.

The CHAIRMAN faid, he had the fatisfaction to acquaint the Court, that this refolution had been fubmitted to the Board of Commiffioners who had agreed to it, and he would beg that the intimation of their concurrence might be read, in order to fhew the opinion the Board entertained on this occafion. The fame was read as follows :

Whitehall, 7th May, 1799.

The Board moft highly approve, and with the greateft pleafure confirm, the refolution of the Court of Directors, requefting the Right Honourable

Rear

Rear Admiral Lord Nelson's acceptance of the fum of 10,000l. as a token of the juft fenfe they entertain of the very important fervices rendered the Eaft India Company, by his Lordfhip's glorious victory over the rench fleet off the Mourh of the Nile, on the firft, fecond and third of Auguft laft; and the Board do not conceive how the Court could have done lefs than they have propofed.

HENRY DUNDAS.
W. PITT.
W. DUNDAS.

The CHAIRMAN informed the Court, that thefe refolutions had been forwarded to Lord Nelfon, through the medium of the Admiralty, the Court having conceived that to be the beft way of communicating to his Lordfhip the fentiments of the Eaft India Company.

Sir *John Cox Hippifley* rofe and faid, that as the Court was exprefsly and originally called for the confideration of Lord Nelfon's fervices, thofe fervices had been fully recognized, and there was but one opinion of their magnitude and importance to the interefts of the Company, he fhould therefore confine himfelf, on the prefent occafion, to fimply moving, that this Court do agree with the refolution of the Court of Directors, in favour of Lord Nelfon, as reported by the Chairman.

This motion being feconded by Mr. W. Lufhington,

The CHAIRMAN obferved, that the motion was not neceffary, as the General Court had referred the bufinefs of remunerating Lord Nelfon to the Court of Directors. He then proceeded to ftate to the Court, that the Directors had come to a refolution of placing the Company's marine forces at Bombay on the fame footing as their army in India, for which purpofe it would be neceffary to bring a bill into Parliament, fubjecting that branch of their fervice to marine law. He believed alfo, it had never been formally announced to the Court, that in the prefent exigency of affairs the Company had thought it right to add a third regiment of their labourers for the protection of their warehoufes.

The CHAIRMAN then ftated, that the Court of Directors having taken into their confideration the fervices rendered to the Company by the late Mr. Edward Hay,

who

who had for many years acted as Secretary to the Government General of Bengal, and had died in diftreffed circumftances, they had been induced, in confideration of his long and eminent fervices, to grant·an annuity of three hundred pounds per annum to his widow, who was left with a family unprovided for, the refolution to which effect would now be fubmitted to the Court for their confideration.

The Clerk then read the proceedings of the Committee of Correfpondence upon the petition of Elizabeth Hay, and their refolution confirmed by the Court of Directors, to recommend it to the General Court, to concur in the grant of an annuity of 300l. per annum to Mrs. Hay, during her widowhood, to commence from May laft.

The CHAIRMAN fpoke in the higheft terms of the long and faithful fervices of Mr. Hay, whofe very extraordinary merits had been confirmed to the Directors by the teftimony of four different Governors General, under whom he had ferved, namely, Mr. Haftings, Marquis Cornwallis, Sir John Macpherfon, and Lord Teinmouth, it having alfo appeared to them that he died in very indigent circumftances, they had from the peculiar nature of the cafe been induced to agree to the application of Mrs. Hay, for a penfion, the refolution to which effect was now fubmitted to the General Court, according to the By-laws, for their fanction.

The CHAIRMAN then moved, that the Court do agree to this refolution, which paffed unanimoufly.

The CHAIRMAN communicated to the Court an application which had been made to the Directors by Mr. George Patterfon to return to India, with his rank in the fervice, with which they had, from the particular hardfhips of Mr. Patterfon's cafe, been induced to comply. As this gentleman had been at home more than five years, it was neceffary that his leave to return fhould be confirmed by the Proprietors. He believed Mr. Patterfon's cafe was well known to moft gentlemen in that Court, he had been reduced to a ftate of indigence by circumftances which it would not be proper to ftate in fo public an affembly. The objections to Gentlemens returning to fituations in the fervice after a long abfence was, that it was injurious to the intereft of thofe fervants who were at prefent difcharging their duty to the Company in India, but in this cafe, fuch was the peculiar good character of the
gentleman,

gentleman, that his re-appointment would give fatisfaction to every member of the fettlement to which he belonged, and his return would be welcomed with open arms. Without entering into the particular circumftances which had occafioned this application, he could affure the Court that Mr. Patterfon was no party to the occurrences which had occafioned the misfortune of the houfe he was connected with,

The Clerk then read the refolution of the Directors for refloring Mr. Patterfon to the Company's fervice.

The CHAIRMAN faid, he would not make any motion upon it, as by the act of Parliament, the confirmation required, which was that of two thirds of the Proprietors, muft be by ballot.

Mr. *Chifholme* begged leave to make one obfervation on the fubject. He did not know Mr. Patterfon, nor did he rife to oppofe his being reflored to the fervice. He thought it however a matter of juftice to the Company's fervants abroad to take fome notice of this meafure. If it had been a new cafe, he fhould make no obfervation upon it, but of late thefe fort of applications had come fo much into practice that they paffed almoft as a matter of courfe. He fhould wave any difcuffion of the fubject in the prefent inftance, but he gave notice that on the next occafion that occured, he fhould rife in his place, and ftate his objections to the principle upon which thefe fort of applications were founded.

The CHAIRMAN obferved, that it did not frequently happen that the Directors brought forward any fuch recommendation ; there were only three inftances of Company's fervants being reflored fince the paffing of the act which gave a difcretionary power to that effect.

Mr. *Chifholme* faid, the inftances had followed each other very clofely, and he thought the practice highly injurious to the fervice.

The CHAIRMAN propofed Tuefday the 2d of July for the ballot on Mr. Patterfon's appointment, which was agreed to.

C ILLICIT

ILLICIT TRADE,

Mr. David Scott.

The Chairman then ftated to the Court, that a part of the bufinefs for which they had been convened, was for confidering a recommendation of the Court of Directors to difpenfe with the prefent By-laws refpecting fhipping, and to permit two fhips to be built upon the bottoms of the Ocean and Henry Addington; and alfo for confidering a Bill propofed to be brought into Parliament for regulating in future the manner in which the Company fhall hire and take up fhips for their fervice; but as the fourteen days notice required by the By-laws had not been given, he would propofe to fix a general Court for the confideration of thofe fubjects, on the 28th June next, which was the earlieft day poffible, and included the time which had elapfed fince the advertifement.

Mr. *Henchman* faid, he did not rife to make any objection to what the Chairman had propofed; but to offer an obfervation, which he hoped he would be admitted to do, refpecting a fubject of great confequence, which he thought ought to make a part of that Bill—he meant the General Trade of India, which, by the Papers that would be before the Court this day, it was evident, was in a ftate that required immediate and very ferious attention. The Bill went to provide for the carrying of that trade, but it did not go into any other regulations, which were moft imperioufly called for. A very wife principle was laid down by the regulating India Act of 1793; but there was the cleareft proof at hand, that merchants had not the neceffary facilities given them under that act, fo as to enable them or the public to benefit to the extent which was intended: the Minifter for India was well aware of this, and would he trufted interpofe; all, Mr. Henchman faid, that he meant to do at prefent, was to give notice, that he or fome of the friends near him would, whenever this Bill came forward, bring the fubject of the General Trade of India into difcuffion, and offer fuch a motion to the Court as fhould tend to affure the Court of Directors and his Majefty's Minifter for India, that they felt the neceffity of fome more effectual regulations being adopted than what at prefent exifted, and that they would moft readily and cordially concur in fuch further encouragement as fhould, after due deliberation, be thought requifite in the prefent ftate of affairs.

The

The CHAIRMAN ftated that in what he had juft before mentioned, " that the " fpecific approbation of the Court of Proprietors was not effential to the validity " of the grant to Lord Nelfon, as it now ftood, he by no means wifhed to be underftood as having confidered their approbation and previous recommendation of the meafure of no importance. He was perfuaded that Lord Nelfon would feel himfelf highly obliged to the Proprietors for the part they had taken in the bufinefs ; all he meant was, that after the Refolution of the Directors had been confirmed by the Board of Controul, it was not regular or neceffary to renew the difcuffion.

Sir *John Cox Hippifley* expreffed himfelf perfectly fatisfied by this explanation, and withdrew his motion.

The CHAIRMAN informed the Court that the notice for taking into their confideration the printed papers on the Illicit Trade of the Company, had been made fpecial at the requeft of an honourable Director, whofe name was alluded to in thofe papers.

Mr. *Scott* faid, that as the honourable Chairman had juft acquainted them, this Court had been made fpecial at Mr. Scott's particular defire, for the difcuffion of a fubject in which he was fo deeply interefted, he would ftate his reafons for having made this requeft, but would not detain them more than a few minutes. The Proprietors had long been in poffeffion of the charges made againft him, and were well acquainted with the enormity of the crimes of which he had been accufed. They had alfo read the Papers on which thefe charges were faid to have been grounded. The whole of thefe Papers had been feveral weeks before them ; it was therefore unneceffary for him to comment upon them at all. The Proprietors had likewife been furnifhed with the minutes of his defence ; thefe minutes he had only delivered in to the Court of Directors a few days ago, having been prevented from fending them fooner by bad health : he ftooped not to recrimination, for he ftood on higher ground. Neither the meafures, nor the motives of his accufer were at prefent in his view. The Papers had no fooner been read in the Court of Directors, on which the charges were founded, than he, Mr. Scott, was exculpated to the complete fatisfaction of the Court, who had acquitted him by an almoft unanimous decifion of every fhadow of imputation.

tation. But, Mr. Scott added, he felt fomething further due to the Proprietors, to the public, and to himfelf: this had occafioned the minutes of defence, and led him this day before them, to requeft their decifion on the fubject. He fought no favour, he only claimed their juftice, and confcious rectitude gave him no anxiety for the refult. He flattered himfelf, that after the heavy imputations caft upon him from fuch a quarter, Gentlemen would think with him, that his calling upon his Conftituents to determine upon his conduct, was as natural as it was right.

Mr. *Chifholme* faid, it was cuftomary on queftions of this kind, to preface any refolution that was brought forward by a long introductory fpeech. He fhould not obferve this method, for it was not his practice to take up for any length of time the attention of the Court. The papers had been printed, and he prefumed, perufed by the Proprietors; he hoped they would think them voluminous enough; he had read them with the utmoft attention, and after he had fo done, he was thoroughly convinced that there was not the leaft foundation for the charges brought forward againft Mr. Scott; he thoroughly acquitted him of every imputation. In faying this, he fpoke from the conviction of his own mind, uninfluenced by any folicitation whatever. When he was thus fully convinced of the innocence of the character of the honourable Director, he felt it to be his duty to bring forward a declaration to that effect; he thought his acquittal ought to be as public and as general as the charge againft him had been made. He felt the time of the Court to be of too much importance to prolong his obfervations, he fhould, therefore, conclude with a fhort refolution, in framing which, he had endeavoured to avoid every thing that might lead to any perfonality; but fhould the debate take any turn which might make it neceffary for him fo to do, he begged leave to claim the privilege of being heard in reply.

Mr. *Chifholme* then moved the following Refolution:

> *Refolved*, That it does not appear to the fatisfaction of this Court from the papers printed for their confideration, that it was neceffary to include the name of David Scott, fenior, in any Bill of Difcovery; but as the Court of Directors have thought proper, at the requeft of Mr. Scott himfelf, (although not confiftent with the refolution of the laft General

neral Court) to prepare a bill including his name, and to submit the same to his Majefty's Attorney General, this Court do acquiefce therein; but they think it incumbent upon them at the fame time to declare, that they do not fee from thefe papers the fmalleft reafon to fufpect Mr. Scott of having betrayed any confidential knowledge, which he poffeffed, as a Member of the Secret Committee, or any part of his duty as a Director of this Company, or of having any perfonal knowledge of the fhip Helfingoer, or of tranfactions relative to the trade of the houfe of David Scott and Co. and that they entirely concur with the Court of Directors, in acquitting him of all perfonal imputation.

Mr. *William Lufhington* rofe to fecond the motion; he wifhed, in common, with every other Proprietor, to contribute to retrieve an highly honourable and refpectable character from the unjuft imputations to which it had been fubjected. He did not mean to arraign the fenfe of duty which had brought forward the charges, but highly as he refpected the author of them, and much as he approved of his general conduct, he could not help expreffing, on this occafion, his aftonifhment that he fhould have entertained and brought forward fufpicions fo unwarranted and unjuft. His only objection to the motion which had been made by his honourable Friend was, that it did not go far enough; he had rifen to fecond it, becaufe fo far as it did proceed, he entirely approved of it, but he regretted that it had not gone farther, for in his opinion, there was not only no grounds of fufpicion againft Mr. Scott, but that there was no foundation for a Bill of Difcovery againft any of the parties implicated in the accufation. The charges, fo far as the honourable Director was concerned in them, prefented three principal and ftriking points, and he had attentively gone through the mafs of papers on which they were founded, without having been able to difcover any folid grounds by which any one of them could be fupported. The firft charge was of a moft ferious nature, that of making public the fecrets of the Company and the State. Mr. Scott and his friends muft neceffarily be anxious to have fo ferious an imputation done away.

The fecond pretends to include Mr. Scott as a partner in the houfe of David Scott, junior, and Co.

The third is an attack upon the houfe of David Scott and Co. difconnected from the name of David Scott, fenior.

In looking over the papers, Mr. Lufhington faid, it was perfectly clear to

D   his

his mind, that there was not a fingle act imputed to the houfe of David Scott and Co. which was not fimply and fairly an act of agency. If in the tranfactions alluded to, the houfe of David Scott and Co. acted on commiffion, it was perfectly fair fo to do, even though the articles purchafed by them for the houfe at Copenhagen might be intended to fupply the enemies of this country. While Government allow imports and exports, it is ftrictly juftifiable in any houfe of agency to act in behalf of foreign neutral nations, on commiffion. The fhip Helfingoer proceeds from hence to Copenhagen; what did her cargo confift of? Articles of Britifh manufacture; fuch articles as it is the bufinefs of Government to protect and encourage the difpofal of; fhe afterwards failed to Manilla, and becaufe the Captain is charged with having faid that he expected to find the place in the hands of the Englifh, it is imputed to Mr. Scott to have given him information of the intention of this country to attack it! And this, though it appears upon the face of the proceedings from whence the charge is made, that the Captain collected his information from a newfpaper put on board his fhip as he paffed through the channel. Mr. Lufhington faid it was unneceffary to dwell on this frivolous charge, which was abandoned by thofe who had brought it forward; he would only add that the fufpicion was moft rafhly adopted. He meant to impute no improper motive to the late Chairman, but he could not help thinking that he had fuffered this groundlefs fufpicion to lay fuch faft hold of his mind that it had perverted his judgment throughout the whole of his inveftigation of the tranfaction. This it was which afterwards led him to convert an act of agency into an act of trading as principal, his mind having once gone the length of fufpecting Mr. Scott of a greater offence, it became eafy to believe him guilty of a leffer; but Mr. Lufhington faid, if, as he had contended, that the tranfactions refpecting the Helfingoer were mere acts of agency, what grounds of imputation were there either againft Mr. Scott, or the Houfe of David Scott, junior, and Co? That the fhip and cargo belonged to the houfe of David Scott and Co. refted folely upon one teftimony, and that one, the evidence of a man, one of the national guards under Roberfpierre; he did not mean to reject his teftimony on this account, but he mentioned it to fhew of what defcription he was, and thence to account for his fubfequent conduct. What had been the conduct of this man, (Rahling)? Firft, he charges his Captain with having been guilty of grofs violence during the voyage, which occafioned the death of two of the feamen. What declaration does he make at this time refpecting the fhip and cargo? He deliberately declares them to be Danifh property;

perty; had they not been fo, his avowed hoftility to the Captain would *then* have led him to have denounced the fhip and cargo Britifh property, and at once to have gratified his revenge and promoted his intereft. But on the contrary, with the fame breath that he complains of the Captain, he declares the fhip and cargo to be Danifh. Afterwards finding he had failed in the ferious charge he had brought forward, of murder, he endeavours by the threat of getting the fhip and cargo condemned as Britifh property, to extort money from the Captain: he fays, in plain terms, give me money and I will abandon the charge. Mr. Lufhington faid, he fhould be glad to know if the oath, the fingle, uncorroborated oath of fuch a man was deferving of any credit? A man, who when difappointed of his object, and after his mind had infenfibly attained a higher pitch of moral guilt, fcruples not to fwear in oppofition to his own previous and deliberate declaration, that the property of the fhip and cargo was in the houfe of David Scott and Co.

Mr. Lufhington faid, he would now proceed to confider, 1ft. whether it could be imputed to Mr. Scott that he had violated his oath of fecrecy to the Company?

2. Whether he could be confidered as a partner in the houfe of David Scott and Co.?

3. Whether any act. was made out againft the houfe of David Scott, and Co. (fetting afide the perjured evidence of Rabling) except acts of agency? He muft repeat that he did not think the motion went far enough; it ought entirely to have annihilated the proceedings for filing a Bill of Difcovery; if they are perfifted in, they will difgrace the Proprietors and the Company in another quarter. Is it probable that the Attorney General (who in this cafe muft be the public profecutor) will act upon refolutions ill underftood and haftily adopted? It cannot efcape him that to difcourage foreign agency is to act againft the true interefis of the country. As long as Government permits the exportation of ftores, it is allowable for Britifh merchants to purchafe them for foreigners, on commiffion; if they ultimately go to Breft, the Agent in this country is not anfwerable; he fends them to his Principal at Copenhagen. He fubmitted to the Court of Directors whether, in order to avoid the difgrace that would attach, if the Attorney General refufed to act upon the grounds haftily adopted by them, it would not be better and wifer to proceed no farther; it was for this reafon he intended to have rifen to make a motion, if his honourable Friend had not. He was fatisfied too, that in juftice to the parties, the profecution ought not to be proceeded on. The Papers which had been printed plainly fhewed, that there was no rational foundation for any imputation either againft Mr. David Scott, fenior, or the Houfe of

David

David Scott and Co. Mr. Lufhington faid, he had recently had occafion as one of a Committee of Weft India merchants, to apply to Minifters for a licence to fend ftores to the Spanifh Weft India Iflands, and his application had been readily granted on the ground of its giving additional vent to the mahufactures of Great Britain. He did not wifh to defend any man whofe conduct was culpable, but he could not but confider Mr. Scott to be wholly unimpeachable, and that the houfe of David Scott and Co. had acted as any other merchant's houfe would, and might have done under the fame circumftances. If there was any doubt as to the right of trading directly with the Spanifh fettlements in the Eaft Indies, he hoped that doubt would fpeedily be removed, and the right eftablifhed. He would fay of this trade as Lord Mansfield had faid of enfuring enemy's fhips, that if it was not law it ought to be ; fo, if during the war the Dutch and Spanifh fettlements in India will trade with us, and their government will permit the intercourfe, he thought it ought to be fanctioned ; it was better fuch a trade fhould centre in Great Britain than with neutral powers. He fhould fay more on this fubject when his hon. Friend (Mr. Henchman) brought forward the difcuffion he had given notice of, and he trufted fome public application would be the refult of it. It fhould never be forgotten that we were not engaged in a common war, on the common motives of hoftility, and that there is a fuperior and imperious policy by which we muft be guided, till the enemy we have to contend with is fubverted and crufhed.

Mr. *Elphinftone* declared, that he rofe under circumftances of great difcouragement. If fuch doctrines as had been laid down by the laft fpeaker were to be adopted, it were better to lock the doors of the India-houfe, and to fhut up their warehoufes, for not a fhadow of their exclufive trade would be left. The honourable Proprietor has told them, that every merchant may act as an agent for fending out goods to the Eaft Indies: he was forry to hear fuch a doctrine admitted in that court to be law. No man in this country could act as an agent in fending out goods intended for India, nor could he legally fend goods to a neutral country, knowing they were afterwards to be fent to India. This was the opinion of the firft lawyers in the kingdom ; and if it was not the law, there did not remain a fhadow of the Company's exclufive trade. He wifhed gentlemen would look at the American treaty. He wifhed the Proprietors would go to the Admiralty Court, as he had done, and hear the decifions of the learned and able Judge, who, happily for the country, fat at the head

of

of that court. There they would find refpectable merchants covering their fhips with direct and pofitive perjury. They had only to write to neutral powers, and for a little money they were inftantly furnifhed with proper papers. A dozen fuch cafes had been proved in the Court of Admiralty in the courfe of the laft month. ' He did not fay this lightly ; but if trade with India was to be carried on under this mafked battery, there would foon be an end of the Company's exclufive privileges. Neutral captains and fupercargoes were always ready at hand, and merchants, to fwear. It was very likely, that during the war the Company might not be fo able to bring home all the produce of India ;- but we ought not, for that reafon alone, to be in hafte to connive at a trade which went to exclude the fair and honeft merchant, and to encourage perfons of a contrary defcription ; perfons who carry on a clandeftine trade, by the medium of foreign flags. Attend to the benefits which are held out to you, as an inducement for fupporting this trade. Who fupported and protected the enemies trade in India ? Thefe refpectable traders, you are told. Who helped to fit out the enemy's fleets there ? Thefe refpectable traders. Who had drained our fettlements of fpecie ? The honourable Gentleman's honourable agents. It was not poffible to conceive a trade more injurious to the interefts of the Company. He begged the Proprietors would paufe, and confider a little the nature and tendency of this trade, and not be led away by fine fpeeches, to do that in an hour which they may repent of for years. The profperity of the Company folely depended on its trade : was that to be parted with for fine fpeeches ? If you part with your trade, there is an end to the profperity of the Company.

· Mr. *William Lufhington* rofe to explain. He faid the honourable Director had miftated his argument. He had fuppofed him to have contended for the right of Britifh fubjects to trade to India as principals. If they purchafe papers of neutral powers, it muft be with a view of covering fuch a trade. There could be no doubt of the illegality of fuch a tranfaction ; and of this complexion he believed the cafes had been, of which the honourable Director alluded to in the Admiralty Courts. As to naval ftores being fent from Great Britain to neutral ports, which ultimately reached the enemy and fupplied their fleets, if Government thought fuch a trade injurious to the country, why did not they ftop it ? The truth is, we cannot monopolize all the military and naval ftores of Europe; and that being the cafe, if the enemy do not obtain them from us, they will get them elfe-

E   where.

where. He agreed indeed with the honourable Director, that if they were not attainable but through us, it would be found policy to forbid their exportation; but as foreign nations would be fupplied at all events, he faw no reafon why we fhould not preferably fupply them.

Mr. *Impey* expreffed his regret, that the queftion of general policy had been introduced into the difcuffion, and fo largely gone into. He thought it would have been more advifeable, not to have fettered the particular tranfaction before the Court with any confideration of that general queftion, which was independent of its merits. In the accufation that had been made, the reputation of a great commercial houfe in the City, and the character and fortune of an honourable Director, had been deeply implicated; and every Gentleman who thought the charge unjuft and unfupported, muft neceffarily feel that fome remuneration was due to thofe who had fuffered under it. In delivering his opinion, he fhould confider himfelf as entering upon a regular judicial enquiry, and as if acting under the fanction of an oath. He meant to make no reflection on the honourable Gentleman with whom the charge had originated. He was perfuaded that the honourable Gentleman himfelf would not now be inclined to fupport the charges he had made, after the light which had, fince he brought them forward, been thrown upon the fubject. He fhould proceed to ftate the evidence as it appeared from the printed papers, fo far as it was connected with the honourable Director (Mr. Scott); from the confideration of which he had been induced to conclude, as the Directors had already done, that there was not the fmalleft reafon to believe the honourable Director implicated in any degree.

The Papers which had been printed were indeed voluminous; but all that related to the fubject now before the Court was contained in a very fmall compafs. The whole charge, as had been well obferved by an honourable Proprietor (Mr. Lufhington), refolves itfelf into the unfupported evidence of Rahling, not only unfupported, but contradicted, by as refpectable men as could be collected to concur in their teftimony of any tranfaction, and contradicted by the only circumftance adduced in its fupport. The charge is this:—That the property of the whole fhip and cargo of the Helfingoer is in David Scott and Co.; not of a *part only*, but the fhip and the *whole* cargo. If, then, there is not a pretence for faying, that the houfe of David Scott and Co. was *concerned in the fhip*; if Rahling is perjured in this part of his evidence, we cannot believe him as to the reft. In oppofition to the oath of Rahling, you have, in the firft place, the fhip's Papers, admitted

admitted on all hands to be regular and authentic, and comprifing the depofition on oath of Mr. Duntzfeldt, (as refpectabie a merchant as any in Copenhagen,) who fwears pofitively, that both the fhip and cargo are his property. You have the oath of Mr. Lennox, a gentleman of unimpeached character, to the fame effect. You have alfo the bill of fale of the fhip, regularly attefted by a Notary Public in London, as executed in his prefence. It appears that this fhip was originally a French prize; that it belonged to an American houfe; was purchafed at Liverpool, by a Mr. Thompfon of Hamburgh, for the houfe of Duntzfeldt, and difpatched from thence to Copenhagen in ballaft. Unlefs thefe papers are forged from the beginning to the end, there can be no doubt of the reality of this tranfaction, and that the houfe of David Scott, junior, and Co. never had any thing to do with the fhip, either as principals or agents. You have alfo the corroboration of the Captain's oath; and with whatever allowance you may accept it, from his intereft in the queftion, it is at leaft equal to Rahling's. But you have alfo Rahling himfelf, who, when folemnly examined before the Governor of Manilla, declares the property of the fhip and cargo to be in Duntzfeldt and Co. The tranfaction refting upon the evidence of Rahling alone, the houfe of David Scott and Co. would ftand acquitted by that declaration in any court in Europe.

There is another circumftance in the evidence of Rahling, of fuch a nature as would of itfelf be completely decifive to invalidate his teftimony. When at laft he declares upon oath the property of the fhip and cargo to be in David Scott and Co. he is afked why he did not make this declaration before? his anfwer is, *he did not think of it*,—an anfwer too much in the ufual ftyle of falfe witneffes to need any comment. But putting the evidence on the other fide, and the prevarications of Rahling entirely out of the queftion, the only circumftance introduced by him into the caufe in fupport of his teftimony is fufficient to deftroy it all. He is afked, how he knew the property of the fhip and cargo to be in David Scott and Co. his anfwer is, he knows it, becaufe he was employed to make out the Danifh invoice from feveral fmall Englifh bills of parcels containing the prices of the articles, the title to which was, " David Scott and Co. Dr." But is it not moft clear from this very circumftance, that the houfe of David Scott and Co. were agents, and not principals. Mr. Impey faid, he fpoke in the prefence of merchants who would correct him, if he drew a wrong conclufion from this fact; but it appeared to him that there would be no end anfwered by fending thefe bills of

parcels

parcels to Copenhagen, but to convince the Houfe there that they had executed the commiffion they were employed upon faithfully.

When the hiftory of the voyage is added to the hiftory of the tranfactions at Manilla, it makes one of the cleareft cafes that ever occurred in a court of juftice. The Captain and Rahling were on terms of hoftility during the whole voyage. During the courfe of it the Captain accufes Rahling of mutiny; on its conclufion Rahling accufes the Captain of murder. Thus the fafety of Rahling and the Captain had become incompatible, and the former tries what he can do to get rid of the latter. Firft he tries to do this by accufing him of cruelty and even murder; when this would not do, he endeavours to ruin him and his own employers by the confifcation of the fhip and cargo. Had he contented himfelf with bringing forward a probable accufation, had he merely faid, that a part of the cargo was Britifh property, for which there might have been fome colour, as part of the cargo is admitted to have been purchafed in London, by the Houfe of David Scott and Co. as agents for Duntzfeldt, he might poffibly have fucceeded; but a part only would not fatisfy his appetite for plunder, and by grafping at the whole, he has luckily for the houfe of David Scott and Co. furnifhed the means of confuting himfelf. But in no way whatever, Mr. Impey faid, was the guilt or innocence of the honourable Director connected with that of the Houfe of David Scott, junior, and Co. except in this, that if they were innocent, it was impoffible for him to be guilty; for admitting Rahling's evidence to be true, for the fake of argument, in its fulleft extent, he would defy any gentleman not acquainted with the charge itfelf, from the Papers which had been printed, as the ground-work of it, to connect Mr. David Scott, the Director, in any manner whatever, with the fhip Helfingoer, the cargo, or the Captain. As to the manner in which Mr. Scott's name had been introduced into the tranfaction, by connecting him with the expectations expreffed by the Captain, he fhould find Manilla in poffeffion of the Englifh, he never heard of fo extraordinary and groundlefs a fufpicion. He could not imagine how fuch an idea could enter into the mind of any man, as to bring forward an accufation on fo flight and frivolous a ground. He meant to impute no improper motive to the late Chairman, but his conduct on this occafion was moft extraordinary. The expedition againft Manilla had been projected here, and orders fent out to India in the Summer of 1796. In the Summer of 1797, the preparations that had been made for it, were known in this country, and all over the world. It was the fubject of daily difcuffion in the newfpapers at that time, and it appears upon the proceedings at the trial, that this very fhip had a newfpaper on board which mentioned the circumftance.

cumſtance. In June 1797, a month before the Helſingoer left Europe, the Go-vernor of Manilla had direct advice from China of the expedition, and was pre-pared to repel it. Mr. Impey aſked whether any fact was brought forward to prove that the communication had been made to the Captain by Mr. Scott. Is' there any evidence of his having ever correſponded with, or been perſonally known to Murray the Captain? At the time the Captain left England, Mr. Scott was then in a diſtant part of the kingdom, five hundred miles from the capital. There is not the ſmalleſt ground for this moſt extraordinary charge of Mr. Scott's having betrayed the Company and his country; and yet, unleſs you do believe this ſuſpicion, you cannot implicate him in the trade, for it is the only fact charged againſt him. As to the proceedings on the Bill of Diſcovery, he could not go ſo far as the worthy Alderman, and agree to put a ſtop to that mea-ſure, as matters now ſtood. If indeed, the Houſe of David Scott and Co. were to apply to the Court of Proprietors, as he perfectly concurred in opinion, that there was not the ſmalleſt ground for entertaining ſuſpicion, he ſhould, when ſo applied to, think it right to ſtop the proceedings. It ſometimes happened, that there was a balance of imputation againſt the acquitted, but in this caſe, after having attentively gone through all the proceedings relative to the ſhip Hel-ſingoer, he was clearly and decidedly of opinion that there was not the ſmalleſt reaſon to impute blame either to the honourable Director or to the Houſe of Da-vid Scott and Co. upon the face of thoſe proceedings.

Mr. *Twining* ſaid, that having called for the printing of the Papers, it would naturally be expected that he ſhould deliver an opinion upon them. He had de-clared at the laſt General Court, that his only motive for printing the papers had been to enable the Proprietors to poſſeſs themſelves of the fulleſt information on the ſubject. They were now produced, and voluminous as they were, he had gone through the whole of them with the utmoſt attention. Before he delivered the opi-nion he had formed, he could not help taking notice of the conduct of the laſt Ge-neral Court, in interpoſing a haſty Reſolution to prevent Mr. Scott's name being included in the Bill of Diſcovery. It was both injudicious and indecorous ; in-judicious as to the honourable Director himſelf, indecorous as to the Court of Directors. The honourable Director was well acquainted with the hiſtory of mankind, and he would aſk him, what conduct an innocent man would have purſued, who was unjuſtly accuſed? Such a man, ſo far from ſhrinking from en-

F   quiry,

quiry, courts it; fo far from flying from profecution, he feeks it. But on the contrary that perfon, who fears that inveftigation may lead to fomething of which he dreads the difcovery, what conduct does fuch a man purfue ? He avoids enquiry, he recedes from profecution. If he cannot do it by his own means, he calls in the aid of friends. Such had been the conduct of the honourable Gentleman's friends at the laft General Court, who had been difpofed to think favourably of him, had difapproved fo entirely of the proceeding, as to withdraw their fupport. A learned Gentleman had complained of the Bill of Enquiry as reftraining the honourable Director in the exercife of his duty; but by the very fame breath in which he enlarges on the hardfhip of reftraining a fingle Director, he makes a motion reftrictive upon the whole Court. The very fame Directors, on the fame day that they cleared the character of Mr. Scott from perfonal imputation, decided on the propriety of including his name in the Bill of Difcovery. If one of thefe Refolutions was to be made invalid, the other ought to have been fo likewife. Mr. Twining afked what the conduct of the Court of Directors would have been, if a Gentleman not concerned with the Direction had been fuppofed to be connected with Illicit Trade ? Whether, inftead of its occupying days, weeks, and months in difcuffing what was proper to be done, meafures would not at once have been taken to difcover the truth and the whole truth ? If fo, it furely was more neceffary, when the character of an Eaft India Director and Merchant was implicated. Of a ftranger we could only complain, that he had injured our commerce. He was not bound to protect it, but a Director is bound, not only not to injure the Company, but to protect and advance its interefts. He muft confider the Refolution of the laft General Court as injurious to the Court of Directors, becaufe it reftrained them from doing what by the tenor of their duty they were bound to do.

Mr. Twining faid, before he obferved upon the printed Papers, he muft notice an expreffion made ufe of by the honourable Director (Mr. Scott) at the laft General Court. He had faid that now there muft be an end either of his own honour or of that of his accufer. He hoped he fhould have the concurrence of the Court of Proprietors when he faid, that he faw no reafon for fo harfh and uncharitable a conclufion. For his part he was perfectly convinced of the pure motives of the late Chairman, though he fhould be reduced to the neceffity of blaming fome part of his conduct, and if he heard it afferted that the honourable Director (Mr. Scott) had no honour, he fhould be as ready to contradict it as any

man.

man. When he thought that hon. Director acted in a manner injurious to the interests of the Company, he was free to say so; but never without giving the grounds of his opinion. As far as he thought his conduct wrong, he would condemn him; but he would not go one jot further. When the Papers upon Illicit Commerce had been referred by his Majesty's Ministers to the late Chairman, he could not do less than promote the enquiry. The alarm given by the Illicit Commerce, which they noticed, had spread itself not only through Europe, but to Asia, Africa, and America. If so called upon he had refused to institute the enquiry, he would justly have deserved to have been reprehended. Having said this he was frank to confess, that in his opinion the late Chairman did not conduct the enquiry in the way that was the most proper. He wished he had not kept it to himself, but had called in the aid of those Directors most calculated from their experience and intelligence to have given him assistance. If indeed the honourable Gentleman had sufficient ground to apprehend that by so doing he should have been over-ruled, and the enquiry suppressed, which he could not suppose would have been the case, he might be justified. If for this or any other motive he had thought proper to conduct the enquiry in his own name, he wished he had made it without bringing forward, in the first instance, such serious and heavy charges, for which there did not appear to be sufficient evidence. He thought he would have acted better, if he had contented himself with merely setting on foot the enquiry. Having said thus much, we ought to recollect, that our situation at this time is different from that in which the late Chairman was placed. We have the result of the enquiries of the Directors, and he dared say, of their well-founded opinion. When the late Chairman first read the Papers, he could not but be extremely struck by the magnitude of the mischief they displayed. He felt, perhaps, a little too much, but we should recollect it was for our interests that he felt, and should not judge him severely. The first branch of the charge accuses the house of David Scott and Co. (which he should always consider the same as David Scott, for a father's interest and his son's was the same) with trading to different parts of Europe and Asia, under the character of Agents, though in fact they were Principals. Before this charge had been made he wished the honourable Gentleman had availed himself of the information of the Members of the Committee to whom the information was referred. Nothing gave him greater satisfaction than being able to say, that so far as it respected the honourable Director's house of commerce, the charge had not in his opinion been

made.

made out. On the contrary it appeared from the Papers, that the houfe of David Scott and Co. did really act as Agents and not as Principals. He alfo thought it was moft clearly fhewn, that the honourable Director had made no fuch communication refpecting the intended expedition againft Manilla, as had been imputed to him. He expreffed this opinion with the more fatisfaction, as he feared the honourable Director or his friends conceived he had fome perfonal ill-will towards him. He folemnly declared, that from the year 1793, when he had firft brought forward a motion affecting the honourable Director, he had never entertained the flighteft ill-will againft him. This he muft add, that he could not but difapprove of the trade, which it was evident had been carrying on for fome time paft. There was nothing more clear than that the property of the enemy had been brought home to Europe by neutral flags, nor than that the houfe of David Scott and Co. (which he confidered the fame as David Scott) did act as Agents to a houfe in Copenhagen, engaged in bringing home that property, nor than that another houfe in Bengal, connected, if not with the houfe of David Scott and Co. was materially concerned in promoting that trade. It was impoffible for him to approve of the honourable Director's interference in that trade ; he even thought lending the influence of his name to fuch tranfactions highly improper ; he had been told that in judging of the conduct of others, we fhould place ourfelves in the fame fituation with thofe whom we arraign. He hoped he fhould be excufed the momentary prefumption of imagining himfelf to be placed behind that Bar, entrufted with the management of the Company's trade, and carrying on at the fame time a feparate commerce of his own of the fame nature ; that after having pretty ftrenuoufly endeavoured to preferve both his fituation as a Director, and his commerce as a merchant, he had been compelled to relinquifh either the one or the other, and in fo doing and abiding by his feat in the Direction, he had placed his infant fon at the head of his houfe of Commerce. He then afked himfelf if he had done fo, what he fhould have thought of his own conduct, and what he fhould have expected the world to think of it ? What could he have thought, or what could the world have thought, but that his withdrawing his name and fubftituting that of his infant fon, was a mere fubterfuge. *Multum intereft qui a quo fiat.* He may have thought right. The time would come when he himfelf and the honourable Director would be no more. If there was enmity on either fide, that enmity would be at an end ; if the influence of friendfhip or power had operated upon the enquiry, that friendfhip would have

ceafed

ceafed, that power would be annihilated. Whenever this period fhould arrive he would venture to fay that there would be but one opinion upon the fubject, and it would become a matter of aftonifhment to future Proprietors, that there ever had been a General Court, who would countenance a Director carrying on at once the concerns of the Company, and engaged either in his own perfon, or his fon's, it mattered not which, in a houfe of extenfive Eaft India agency. Mr. Twining faid, with refpect to that part of the refolution which had been moved, and which went to confirm the refolution of the Directors, acquitting Mr. Scott of perfonal imputation, he had not the flighteft objection to it. As to that part which alluded to withdrawing the hon. Director's name from the Bill of Difcovery, he muft object to that, and he begged leave to fupport his objection by alluding to the opinion of the Attorney and Solicitor General on the papers referred to them. They had ftated, that though they did not contain precife grounds for a profecution, they excited ftrong fufpicions, which due diligence might bring to light. With this opinion before us, faid Mr. Twining, fhall we ftop enquiry? It would be moft impolitic to do fo. Nor is it neceffary; for the honourable Director himfelf has, fince the laft General Court, defired that his name may be included in the Bill of Difcovery. The motion therefore goes unneceffarily far. If however it is to be fuffered to pafs in its prefent form, he fhould think it right immediately after to move another, fimilar to that which had paffed the Court of Directors, expreffing the fenfe of the Court of the integrity of their late Chairman, and thanking him for his conduct.

Mr. *Impey* afked, whether the opinion to which the honourable Proprietor had alluded was not given upon the Papers generally, and not upon Mr. Scott's cafe, which was the matter now before the Court?

Mr. *Twining* faid, it was enough for his argument if it was given on the Papers generally, which included Mr. Scott's cafe.

Mr. *Watfon* faid, the candour and liberality with which the honourable Proprietor, who had juft fat down, had conducted himfelf that day muft meet with the concurrence and approbation of every body. As an individual wholly unconnected with any party, he could not give a filent vote on this occafion. He did not entirely agree with the motion as it now ftood. The honourable Gentleman

G

tleman who brought it forward had properly obferved that the acquittal **ought** to be as public and as general as the accufation. After his learned Friend had gone fo completely and ably through the evidence, there could not be a doubt as to the innocence of David Scott, fenior. That being the cafe, he could not agree to the fuggeftion which fell from the learned Alderman. He thought it not right to go through the whole of the Papers, and that part of his obfervations was irrelevant to the queftion. He had faid that he thought fome difgrace would attach on the Court of Proprietors if the King's Attorney General did not agree with them in opinion, and had urged this as a reafon for coming to an immediate decifion againft the Bill of Difcovery. He felt the greateft refpect for the Proprietors of India Stock, but he fubmitted whether, after the Attorney General had been furnifhed with the documents, after the honourable Director had requefted that he might be made a party to the Bill, when an appeal was about to be made to one of the higheft tribunals in the country, would it be decorous in the Court to decide judicially upon the queftion ? He was perfuaded the late Chairman, in the conduct he had purfued, had beeen actuated by zeal for the credit of the Company. There might have been *prima facie* evidence to ground his charge upon. Thinking there was, he had manfully ftepped forward. He would not now enquire whether the mode he had purfued was fuch as he approved. The honourable Proprietor, who had called for the printing of the Papers, had candidly admitted, after fifting the matter to the bran, that there was no ground of imputation againft the honourable Director, except for having placed his infant Son in his houfe of agency. From this act Mr. Watfon drew a different conclufion from the honourable Proprietor, and thought it proved to demonftration that it was an actual change of property, and not a colourable relinquifhment privately fabricated in the clofet for finifter purpofes; that the honourable Director in the face of the world had divefted himfelf, and vefted in truftees all his property in the houfe, beyond the power of redemption, intending fairly and honourably to have done with the houfe altogether. Having anfwered that part of the argument he fhould only obferve as to the words of the motion, that he thought it would be better to confine it to what went to approve of the Refolution of the Directors acquitting Mr. Scott.

Mr. *W. Lufhington* faid, that the learned Gentleman had mifunderftood the firft part of the motion, and begged it might be read, which being done,

Mr.

Mr. *Watfon* faid, his only objection was removed, and he perfectly concurred.

Mr. *Randle Jackfon* faid, he could not concur in the thanks that had been lavifh-ed by his learned Friend on the hon. Proprietor, who had originally moved for the printing of the Papers, for his extraordinary candour and liberal line of conduct. Feeling himfelf compelled, by the force of truth, to acquit the honourable Director of the heavy and unfounded charges brought againft him, he had thought fit to accom-pany his acquittal with much dark and dangerous infinuation. He had fo interwo-ven it with heavy imputations on the character of the honourable Director, that he ftood almoft as much affected by thofe infinuations as by the imputations which he profeffed to exonerate him from. If the honourable Director was innocent, let him be declared fo unequivocally. If he thought him guilty, it was the honour-able Gentleman's duty, who had called for the Papers, to move for his difmiffion ; but furely it was not candid to accompany his acquittal by fuch infinuations. Would this fort of acquittal fatisfy Mr. Scott's mind ? Would it fatisfy his friends ? Every newfpaper contained paragraphs goading him to a ftep, which Mr. Jackfon regretted that he had taken, that of defiring to have his name in-cluded in the Bill of Difcovery. This he had endeavoured at the laft General Court to prevent, becaufe he thought it vexatious and oppreffive. He was aftonifh-ed that the hon. Proprietor had treated the conduct of the laft General Court as un-juft and indecorous ; as if a motion, which had been founded in truth and juftice, had been carried by the mere influence of private friendfhip. It was not the ob-ject of that motion, nor the terms of it, to prevent profecution, where profecution could be made the medium of difcovery. All that had been faid to the Directors, by that motion, was, " While you confefs, on your own records, that Mr. Scott is innocent, do not treat him as if he was guilty. So long as you declare that Mr. Scott knows nothing, why file a Bill againft him for difcovery?" The words of the motion gave a latitude to the Directors, if they faw reafon to revoke their opinion, to proceed accordingly ; but the honourable Proprietor had uncandidly argued as if avoiding a Bill in Chancery was of itfelf a decifive proof of guilt. Any man, who knew the delay and vexations of a court of law, might dread a fuit impending over him, and yet be perfectly innocent of the fubject of that fuit. There were other modes of proving innocence befides that of voluntarily becom-ing a defendant to a Chancery fuit. How had Mr. Scott conducted himfelf ? Had he fhrunk from enquiry ? No. He had always promoted it ; it was he who

had

had fuppoited a general inveſtigation of the Illicit Trade ſaid to be carried on, before it was known whom it might implicate. He had repeatedly challenged and intreated publicity, as ſoon as it was hinted that himſelf was a party ; he had met the charge by a moſt ſolemn and inſtant denial upon oath before God and the magiſtracy ; he had ſince refuted it article by article ; he had profeſſed his readineſs to anſwer any queſtion which courts or committees might propound to him ; to produce to them any papers which they might require, or to reveal to them every particular of his arrangement with his late houſe, of however private or delicate a nature ; but both himſelf and his friends had ſeen the drift of the propoſed Bill of Diſcovery. They ſaw it was to reſtrain, if not ſuſpend, his directorial functions, and prevent him from being a Candidate for the Chair. The laſt General Court had ſeen it in the ſame light ; they had detected the ſecret purpoſe of Mr. Scott's adverſaries, and, having detected it, were determined to prevent it. But how had they prevented it ? Not by coming down to Court as the honourable Proprietor had inſinuated, like a mob of hirelings, to ſcreen Mr. Scott from enquiry ; but a large majority of a moſt reſpectable General Court had, after eight hours diſcuſſion, ſaid to the Directors, in terms conſonant to truth and juſtice :
" We are averſe to making a proſecution the medium of perſecution. You de-
" clare, by a great majority, that Mr. Scott is innocent ; and yet ſeveral of you
" propoſe to proſecute him as if he were guilty. You declare your conviction
" that he is totally ignorant of the tranſactions in queſtion ; and yet you propoſe
" to file a Bill againſt him to compel a diſcovery of thoſe very tranſactions. We
" deſire you not to haraſs Mr. Scott in courts of law, till you ſhall ſee reaſon to
" revoke your reſolutions of acquittal, or at leaſt till we have peruſed the Papers
" propoſed to be printed, and enabled ourſelves to judge of the premiſes." Thoſe Papers were now before the Court ; the honourable Proprietor had been allowed time ſufficient to make himſelf maſter of their contents, and he was now called upon for his verdict of guilt or acquittal ; but it ſhould be unequivocally one or the other ; it ſhould be no cold acquittal ; it ſhould be a verdict that the world could underſtand, and that as publicly delivered as the charges had been made. If the Directors had changed their opinions ſince their reſolution of acquittal, let them declare it. If cauſe of ſuſpicion had ſubſequently ariſen, let them ſhow it ; and he would now conſent to a Bill being filed, but he would not without cauſe being ſhewn. It was true that Mr. Scott had, ſince their laſt meeting, of himſelf deſired to be included in the Bill ; and now this very conceſſion was argued as a proof

of

of guilt, and a mere anticipation of what he would otherwife have been forced
to fubmit to ! He thought Mr. Scott ought not to have made this conceffion;
he honoured, however, his fenfibility, while he took the liberty to condemn
what appeared to him a want of prudence ; it was notorious that the honourable
Director had been goaded into this meafure ; when other artifices had failed, he
had been goaded by paragraphs in newfpapers, which imputed Mr. Scott's acceptation of the protection of the General Court to his fear of inveftigation ; he
had been goaded by fuch arguments as the honourable Proprietor had that day
ufed ; fuch as, that guilt flies from enquiry, and innocence courts it! Could
the honourable Proprietor conceive no other criterion of innocence than its
courting a Bill in Chancery, which Mr. Scott (whofe life he hoped, for the fake
of the Public, would be a long one) might not live to fee an end to ? Was it no
proof of innocence to challenge publicity, and tender himfelf to perfonal interro-
gatory, as the honourable Director had done ? Some fymptoms of what he had
to expect from a Bill in Chancery had already difcovered themfelves ; for only
fince Mr. Scott had expreffed his confent to be included in one, it had been
fought to add other fubjects of difcovery, and fo it might go on to the end of the
longeft life. Since, however, Mr. Scott (unable to exift under the calumnies
that had been heaped upon him) had requefted to have a Bill of Difcovery filed
againft him, in order to remove them ; Mr. Jackfon faid he faw no alternative for
the Court but to agree to it. But he could not help calling upon the Directors, individually and generally, as men of honour, to take care that no unneceffary delay
fhould be fuffered to interpofe itfelf; and fince they had not thought proper to
interpofe between Mr. Scott and his fenfibility, (as he thought they fhould have
done) he hoped they would be mindful how effential it was to Mr. Scott's peace,
that the bufinefs fhould be brought to a fpeedy iffue. He repeated his regret
at the ftep which Mr. Scott had taken, he thought the General Court had furnifhed him with an anfwer, that ought to fatisfy every liberal mind, namely, that
the Directors were only enjoined to be confiftent, but were at liberty to file a
Bill againft him the moment they would declare there was ground for fufpicion.
Accufation was of itfelf a ferious thing, and it might have occurred to the honourable Proprietor, that it was poffible for a man to be repeatedly accufed, and
yet be innocent—that a Director might be charged with perjury and mutilation
of oaths, and yet be declared innocent by his very accufer. The honourable
Proprietor furely could not have forgotten the very ferious charges which he

himfelf

himfelf had brought, at different times, againft Mr. Scott. In the year 1794, the honourable Gentleman had charged him, in terms impoffible to mifunderftand, not only with having traded contrary to his oath as a Director, but with having clandeftinely altered the terms of an oath, in its way from the General Court to Parliament, in order to accommodate it to the trade, which he fuppofed the honourable Director to carry on. The honourable Gentleman had printed the fpeech which contained this charge, and circulated it from one end of the land to the other, while the honourable Director was in a diftant part of Britain, and before he could have time to explain the circumftance. When the honourable Director returned to town, and enquiry was made as to the fact, it turned out, that Mr. Scott did not even know that the oath had been altered, but that the Directors themfelves had defired the Solicitor to the Company and his honourable Friend, Mr. Henchman, to fhape the words of the oath to meet what was believed to be the fenfe of a previous refolution of a General Court. He had the pleafure afterwards to hear the honourable Proprietor, in his place, admit his miftake, and regret that he had wounded the honourable Director's feelings. —Wounded them, indeed, faid Mr. Jackfon !—A charge fo generally publifh- ed, and fanctioned by a name fo refpectable, as was that of the honourable Pro- prietor, muft have funk and deftroyed any man, the worth of whofe character was lefs known than Mr. Scott's.

The ill fuccefs of this charge had not, however, difcouraged the honourable Proprietor, who, fome time after, brought another charge againft Mr. Scott, as continuing to be indirectly concerned in a houfe of Indian agency, contrary to a recent By-Law. It was known that in 1795, a By-Law had paffed, prohibit- ing Directors from trading to India, as principals or agents. This, though a wife and falutary law, and one that had his warm fupport, was, as to the then Directors, an *ex poft facto* law.

Mr. Scott was, at that time, as were feveral other Directors, concerned (as lawfully they then might be) in houfes of Eaft India agency ; and they had to choofe between relinquifhing their feats in the direction, or their agency concerns. Mr. Scott's, as being the largeft concern, was of courfe the moft lucrative; but he chofe rather to relinquifh it, than to relinquifh a feat, of which he was fo juftly proud, from its having been repeatedly, and in the moft flattering way, con-
ferred

ferred upon him by the Proprietors. It was true that Mr. Scott had not given away his valuable concern to a stranger, but to the son for whom he had always intended it, and, who being a minor, Mr. Scott had vested it in trustees for his benefit ; and the only question that could arise was, whether or no this was a *bona fide* relinquishment ? The honourable Proprietor had charged that it was not, and had (as he had a perfect right to do) brought it before the General Court, upon the eve of Mr. Scott's last election ; the question was then solemnly dif-cuffed in a crowded Court, when it appeared that Mr. Scott had *irrevocably* alienated all right, title, interest, and control, in and over his late concern ; that he had done so under the guidance of the Attorney and Solicitor General, and other eminent Lawyers ; and that Mr. Rous, the Company's Counsel, had declared his conviction that it was a *bona fide* relinquishment ; and that he knew nothing more which Mr. Scott could do to satisfy the law. The Court were of the same opinion, and declared their entire satisfaction by a great majority ; and their opinion that Mr. Scott had no commercial interest whatever, which affected his eligibility to a seat in the Direction.

One would have expected that a subject so fully and repeatedly canvassed, might at last have found rest ; but the honourable Proprietor had again stirred its embers, and broadly hinted that Mr. Scott still retained an interest in his late commercial house, contrary to law. If the honourable Proprietor still entertained doubts upon that subject, or if he had arrived at further information, would he propose a day for its discussion, and, Mr. Jackson said, he would second the motion ; but he would never suffer the honourable Proprietor, or any other per-son in that place, to scatter insinuations against the characters of their Directors, without calling on them to make specific charges.

The honourable Gentleman had, indeed, on that day, gone still further, and almost charged Mr. Scott with being cognisant of certain transactions in the house of Fairlie and Co., of Bengal, alledged to be illicit, and this with the same breath that he compulsively pronounced his acquittal upon the present occasion. Either the honourable Gentleman ought to support his accusations, or to forbear his insinuations. If either of them were true, Mr. Scott ought, with all their affection for him, to be driven from his seat. As for the honourable Gentleman's vote of acquittal, Mr. Scott thanked him not for it. Mr. Scott

owed

·owed his acquittal to his cafe ; it was to be found in the documents which had been publifhed ; and, Mr. Jackfon faid, he defired the whole Court, and the whole Public to underftand, that Mr. Scott's friends would enter into no compromife ; but that they dared and defied accufation, as to any part of his conduct.

This, Mr. Jackfon faid, naturally brought him to confider the charges immediately before them, which, as Mr. Scott had obferved in his Minute of Defence, refolved themfelves into three diftinct heads, viz. High Treafon—Traitorous ·Correfpondence—and Illicit Trade.

The firft and third charge had been fo fully difcuffed by his honourable Friends, that he fhould fay but little upon them. To the fecond charge he fhould ftill lefs fay, as Mr. Scott's name did not even appear in fact, or by allufion, throughout the voluminous Papers to which that charge could alone be referred. Mr. Jackfon faid, he defired it to be recollected, that they were diftinct and abfolute *charges*. He had feen a Paper lately put in by Mr. Bofanquet, which foftened the term down to *opinions*, and which made all the difference. Had the late Chairman, when he laid the Papers before the Court, accompanied them in the ufual way, by his verbal opinions, and left his colleagues to deliberate and act upon them, he for one, fhould have thanked and applauded his vigilance ; but when he found, that inftead of fo doing he had, in the firft inftance, placed upon the Records of the Company charges of fo heavy a nature againft one of their Executive Body, he could not help cenfuring his conduct, in this inftance, as moft rafh, intemperate, and unjuft. He wifhed to advert as little as poffible to the conduct of the late Chairman in this bufinefs, for whom he entertained great perfonal refpect. He believed fuch to be the difpofition of his friends, nor would they be induced to depart from that line of conduct, unlefs an honourable Proprietor (Mr. Twining) fhould think it difcreet to perfevere in a motion, which he had intimated his intention to bring forward when that before the Court fhould be difpofed of.

The charge of high treafon, Mr. Jackfon faid, it would have been impoffible to treat with gravity, but for the quarter from which it had originated—the whole of it was founded upon the polluted teftimony of a fet of infamous

famous vagabonds—vagabonds upon their own fhewing, vagabonds according
to the adjudication of the Spanifh Courts, vagabonds according to the opinion
of their own ftanding Counfel, who, with the candour which belonged to his
character, had fpoken of them as witneffes deferving of reprobation and re-
proach ; and even the evidence of thefe mifcreants was but hearfay evidence,
viz. that they had heard Capt. Murray fay, that he expected to find Manilla
in the hands of the Englifh.—Could one read, without fmiling, this fpeech of
Murray's imputed to Mr. Scott's having violated his oath of fecrefy, by im-
parting the intention of the Britifh Government to Captain Murray, in order
that he might impart it to the Spanifh Governor of Manilla ? The charge was
extravagant enough in itfelf, but that had come out in evidence which rendered it perfectly ludicrous ; the fource of Murray's prognoftics had been trac-
ed, a common Englifh newfpaper found on board, and delivered up among
other papers to the Spanifh Court of Admiralty, which fpoke of the certainty
of the capture of Manilla ; indeed it was notorious that both Manilla and Batavia had been taken by anticipation from a very early part of the war ; fo notorious, that the report of the premeditated attempt had reached Manilla, and
become ftale even there, fome months before the arrival of Murray with the
fhip Helfingoer. The Helfingoer failed from Copenhagen for India in July,
1797. In a letter from the Philippine Company at Manilla, dated October,
1797, they fpeak of a former letter which they had written to Europe, dated
Auguft, 1797, in which they fpoke of accounts which they had received from
Canton in the preceding June, of an intended expedition againft their fettlement, but which they fay is now out of the queftion, fince the monfoons are
fet in. And yet it was with thefe papers lying before him, that Mr. Bofanquet had charged the intelligence to have proceeded from Mr. Scott, though
it might have occurred to him, that if true, Mr. Scott muft be a fool as well
as a traitor, if he were interefted in the cargo, as he was alledged to be, fince
he would be fending that and himfelf into the jaws of feizure and difcovery !
To enlarge further upon the defence on this head, would be as abfurd as the
charge.

The fecond charge of traiterous correfpondence, by fupplying the enemy
with military as well as other ftores, was, if poffible, ftill more extravagant and
unfounded.—This charge could only apply to what was called the Batavia

J   tranfactions,

tranſactions, reſpecting which a liſt of very eminent houſes had been inſerted in the charge, and amongſt the reſt that of David Scott and Co. How would thoſe who had not read the Papers be aſtoniſhed to hear, that from one end of thoſe Papers to the other, the name of David Scott. ſingly, nor even the firm of David Scott, jun. and Co. did not once appear! This fact rendered ſuperfluous all further comment.—A charge was made, certain Papers were referred to in ſupport of it, and in thoſe Papers, the party charged was not even alluded to! To ſay more upon this part of the ſubject would be abuſing the indulgence of the Court. He muſt admit indeed that at the preſent moment Mr. Scott's name did ſtand connected with the Batavian Papers, and by means, in his humble judgment, not the moſt ingenuous. A paper (as if to cover the flagrant abſurdity of bringing forward papers in ſupport of a charge which bore no alluſion to the accuſed) had been ſince hitched into the caſe laid before their Counſel under the grave denomination of " the ſubſequent examination of Mr. Swinton ſince his arrival in England," an examination taken the Lord knows where, and by the Lord knows who! And of courſe an examination altogether *ex parte*, and under no legal obligation as to its truth; this paper had been faſtened upon the Batavia papers, though it was no document from India or St. Helena, though it was no document even of the Eaſt-India Company's, it had no place upon their records. If the Court of Directors had authoriſed ſuch an examination, it ſhould ſeem as if they declined its acknowledgment, for he could find nothing in their minutes which indicated its permiſſion or its acceptation. Mr. Jackſon ſaid he reprobated more the manner of obtaining this paper, and the evident intention with which it was obtained, than the matter it contained; for it did not weigh a feather in the ſcale. Who this Mr. Swinton was, he would not at that moment enquire, but his character as it appeared upon the proceedings in the Court of Admiralty could not altogether have eſcaped an honourable Director (Mr. Elphinſtone) whoſe buſineſs led him to a pretty frequent attendance upon that Court.

The third and laſt charge, namely, that of Illicit Trade, he admitted, as it had been well deſcribed by the Directors in the courſe of the proceedings to be a charge of a very popular nature—cry out Contraband Trade! and an inſtant confuſion of ideas ſeemed to take place in the minds of many perſons; it was a key that artful men ſeldom had or would fail to touch with advantage. To talk.

with

with people out of doors upon this fubject, one would fuppofe that no European Power but the Britifh had a foot of land in India: they feemed to confound and huddle together the principles of national and municipal law, and to forget that Englifh merchants might not only lawfully but laudably export Britifh manufactures, and imports, either as principals or agents, to Copenhagen, Lifbon, or to the European territories of any other Power with whom we are at peace—and that the foreign merchant might again as lawfully export thofe fame commodities to their own Indian fettlements, or to thofe of their friends and allies; and yet this propofition comprized the whole of the cafe even againft the houfe of David Scott, ⬛ and Co.

Mr. Jackfon faid he had given the Papers moft ferious attention; and he protefted he could not fee the grounds which juftified the Directors proceeding even againft the houfe, and he was happy to find himfelf fupported in that opinion not only by his honourable Friends (Mr. Lufhington and Mr. Impey) but by the honourable Proprietor himfelf, to whom he had had occafion to allude. He fhould not enlarge on this topic, as it was not the houfe of David Scott, jun. and Co. but David Scott, fen. who ftood accufed before them. He could not however help affuring himfelf, that the Directors would paufe and ferioufly confider before they added to the difcredit which had been prematurely brought upon that eminent and highly refpectable houfe, without they indeed faw moft unequivocal grounds for fufpicion. But even admitting, for argument's fake, that David Scott, jun. and Co. had been guilty of contraband trade, the fingle queftion before the Court under this head of charge was, whether or no David Scott, fen. was interefted in, or cognifant of, thofe tranfactions?—The General Court had upon a former occafion, folemnly declared their conviction that he did not retain the fmalleft connection with, or intereft in, his former concern: The Court of Directors had recently, repeatedly, and almoft unanimoufly, declared that he had no knowledge of, or intereft in, the tranfactions of that houfe, and that therefore they acquitted Mr. Scott from all perfonal imputation.—The anfwer which the motion before the Court required from the Proprietors, was, did they or not agree with their Directors? In other words, was Mr. Scott innocent or guilty? If, after having perufed and attended to the difcuffion of the Papers, the Court thought him guilty, let there be no blinking of the queftion, let them boldly declare fo, and act upon that declaration!—But if, on the contrary, they

thought

thought him innocent, he conjured them as men of honour, he called upon them by all the fympathies which men of character fhould feel for each other, men that knew the high value of unfullied reputation to themfelves and to their pofterity, and who could feel for the poignant fufferings, and meafure the calamity which attended its impeachment, to pronounce Mr. Scott's acquittal publicly, decidedly, and unanimoufly!

Mr. *Twining* faid, the learned Gentleman, who had laft fpoken, had addreffed his obfervations fo pointedly to him, that he hoped he fhould be indulged with a few words in reply. He believed, after what the Court had witneffed, they would be inclined to think that it required no common fhare of patience, confcious as he was of his own innocence, to fit ftill under fuch heavy imputations. The learned Gentleman began by ftating that he (Mr. Twining) had been compelled to deny an affertion which he had made in that Court. To this he would only anfwer, that he really underftood him not. He was fure that he had never retracted any thing that he had either faid or publifhed as a fact. Though the learned Gentleman always fpoke with great force and energy, he hoped the Proprietors would not fuffer themfelves to be mifled by profeffional eloquence, and that he fhould be protected by them from profeffional language fo exceedingly ftrong. Speaking of the Refolution of the laft General Court, he ftates it to have been formed after a debate of eight hours. It fhould be recollected that the Proprietors on that day were convened upon bufinefs of a very different nature. Four hours of the eight were occupied on the grant to Lord Nelfon, and four hours on the debate enfuing, of which no previous notice had been given. The learned Gentleman accufes the by-law, to prevent Directors trading, with being an *ex poft facto* law. He could not conceive how it was fo. By-laws are made when the neceffity for them arifes. It furely was not *ex poft facto* with reference to Mr. Scott, for Mr. Twining faid he had himfelf, when he brought forward the by-law, propofed that the honourable Director fhould be allowed till December 1797 to wind up every tranfaction with the Houfe. There furely was nothing fevere in this mode of procedure The by-law itfelf had been fanctioned under circumftances fo ftrong as had, Mr. Twining faid, been highly flattering to him, and fuch as he fhould always reflect upon with fatisfaction. But it feemed the learned Gentleman was offended becaufe he had alluded to the connection which Mr. Scott held in the Houfe of David Scott and Co. by having his infant Son at the head of it, after it had been

decided

decided by Proprietors that he had no interest. He certainly continued of the same opinion he liad expreffed before that decifion, that the intereft of the Son was the fame with that of the Father. Does the honourable and learned Gentleman recollect how often he has combated againft repeated decifions in that Court, refpecting the fhipping concerns of the Company ? Yet he thought, and thought rightly, that he might, notwithftanding fuch decifions, bring the fubject forward again in any way he might think fit. Decifions may be obtained in fuch a manner as to render them in no way either impofing or convincing.

Mr. *Durant* faid, he was of the defcription of perfons appealed to by the honourable Proprietor for their opinion ; a plain fpoken, independent man, not poffeffing any profeffional talents. On fuch an occafion as the prefent, he felt it incumbent on him not to give a filent vote, more efpecially as he had taken part in the difcuffion, at the laft General Court, the refult of which had been fo much complained of by the honourable Proprietor. He had fupported the Refolution of fufpending all proceedings at law againft Mr. Scott, till the Directors themfelves fhould be of opinion that there were fome grounds for fuch a meafure. He had done fo becaufe he had experienced the injury which the character of the honourable Director had undefervedly fuffered from the hafty and unfupported charges that had been made againft him. When the terms of thofe charges were known on the Royal Exchange, and by what high authority they had been brought forward, he declared, that nineteen out of twenty of thofe he had fpoken to were ftrongly prejudiced againft Mr. Scott ; and fo deep-rooted was the impreffion, that he found great difficulty, even now, that his innocence was as clear as the fun, to beat it out of their heads. He thought, though he was no lawyer, that if he heard a cafe fully ftated, by both parties, he was capable of deciding who was right and who was wrong. He had liftened to both parties, and had heard and read all that had been faid and written on the fubject ; and he did, in his confcience, believe, that there was no ground for the accufation. He had had the fatisfaction of hearing the two Gentlemen, the accufer and the accufed, plead their own caufe. It was a very different thing from the fpeech of a man who was hired to ftate a cafe. He fhould not deferve the name of an Englifhman, if, after fuch information, he was not able to form an opinion. He had a moft decided one, and it was, that David Scott was an injured man, and was in the right. He differed widely from the honourable Proprietor who had fpoken laft, who had argued as if

K   a Bill

a Bill in Chancery was a mere wind whiftling through a key-hole, a thing of
courfe, not in the leaft vexatious or worth avoiding. He knew to the contrary.
He had himfelf had a Bill in Chancery hanging over his head for feven years,
and had fuffered thoufands of painful hours through the fubtleties of lawyers,
though their dexterity had not been able ultimately either to diminifh his purfe
or affect his character. He hoped, on this occafion, there would be but one opinion. He had not heard one man ftand up in the Court to juftify the late Chairman, or to condemn Mr. David Scott, except the honourable Proprietor who had
laft fpoken. He fhould not exprefs all he thought of the accufation itfelf, or the
mode of conducting it, becaufe it was a rule with him, on all occafions, to avoid
perfonality. If any Gentleman would force him to a perfonal altercation, he muft
get out of the fcrape as well as he could. He was furprized to hear the honourable Proprietor who fpoke laft, whom he had always confidered to be a candid man,
poffeffing a great deal of the milk of human kindnefs, fo pointed and perfonal as he
had been in his obfervations on the proceedings of the laft General Court. He had
afked a learned friend, who fat near him, whether he was ftrictly in order in doing
fo, for he conceived to the contrary. The honourable Gentleman had began his
fpeech by condemning the conduct of the laft General Court, where the attendance
had been very numerous and refpectable, in terms the moft indecorous. He
had fpoken of them as if they had been packed together to carry Mr. Scott through
thick and thin, right or wrong. Mr. Durant declared, for his part, his vote was
not to be bought or biaffed, and he gave other Gentlemen credit for acting with
equal independence. In the fecond divifion of his fpeech, the honourable Proprietor had faid, there were two characters before the Court ; one of them, that of
the late Chairman, he had pronounced to be pure and immaculate. He had
liftened a great while in hopes that he would have paid a fimilar compliment to
the integrity of the other Gentleman, but not a word had fallen from him to pronounce Mr. Scott's character to be pure and immaculate. In his opinion, Mr.
Durant faid, the motives of Mr. Scott were as pure as thofe of any other man.
He gave the late Chairman credit for good intention, but he was not clear that
purity of motive was all that was neceffary to entitle a man to fill high ftations,
or to juftify the errors he might commit in the difcharge of his functions. High
ftations called for fuperior abilities to fill them, and any man who undertook a
refponfible office, affecting the interefts of others, without adequate talents or
judgment, ought to be prapared with fome better plea in his vindication than

purity

purity of motive. If, for inftance, his Majefty, which, by the by, was not very likely, chofe to difmifs Mr. Pitt, and make him Prime Minifter, though he would not yield even to Mr. Pitt in purity of motive, yet, for want of equal abilities, he might by his blunders ruin the country in lefs than a twelvemonth. Would the country be fatisfied, after he had brought it into fuch a dilemma, with his pleading his well-meaning ignorance in juftification of his abfurd politics? He believed not.—Mr. Durant faid it was very evident that he fhould not be completely exonerated even by the honourable Proprietor himfelf; for, while he had applauded the motives of the late Chairman, he had pretty ftrongly cenfured his conduct. That honourable Proprietor had ftated the inveftigation to refolve itfelf into three propofitions; of the two heavieft, affecting the property and' life of the honourable Director, he had completely acquitted him. What was the only charge that remained in that honourable Gentleman's opinion? That he was the father of David Scott, junior, a minor, from whence he chofe to infer that Mr. David Scott, the Director, ftill carried on, or was interefted in the bufinefs of the Houfe, and he perfifted in thinking either that the one fhould never be a merchant, or the other never a Director. He thinks it utterly inconfiftent that a Director, who is the father of a merchant, fhould difcharge his duty to the Company with fidelity, as if a man could not at once be faithful to his conftituents, and affectionate to his child, but muft neceffarily make a facrifice of his public duty to his domeftic attachments. If fo, why not exclude thofe from the direction whofe daughters were married to merchants? The private tie was nearly as forcible. But this is a doctrine in which he will never be fupported in the City or elfewhere. Upon the whole, Mr. Durant faid, that the fpeech of the honourable Proprietor was one of the moft extraordinary, and uncandid he had ever heard. It was replete with infinuation that contained no charge but one, unnaturally linked to acquittal, and while it endeavoured to convey a great deal of cenfure to the mind of the Proprietors, it contained no fpecific charge but one, which was, that Mr. David Scott, the Director, was the father of a merchant. Under thefe circumftances he could not but confider the honourable Proprietor as a very feeble opponent of the motion before the Court, and he believed, from the obfervations he had made of the fentiments of the Court in general, he would be the only opponent.

Mr. *Peter*

Mr. *Peter Moore* faid, he thought they were convened for the fpecial purpofe of confidering certain Papers which had been printed, in purfuance of a Refo- lution of a General Court of Proprietors, on the fubject of Illicit Trade. But, the Court was very unexpectedly involved in the difcuffion and confideration of a perfonal queflion. It was not poffible, Mr. Moore faid, that any Proprietor could deprecate the difcuffion of perfonal queflions more than he did : their meetings there were for very different objects and interefts : but his embarraff- ment was confiderably and painfully encreafed when the pofition, in which they were placed, threatened to leave no alternative between the condemnation of one party or the other ; both of whom urged honeft conduct and difinterefled mo- tives, and confequently laid ftrong claim to their attention and protection. Hence Mr. Moore hoped and trufted, and ftrongly urged, that fome middle way might be hit off, honorable to both parties, that might carry unanimity on the one fide the Bar, and remove the prefent agitated caufes of divifion on the other. In times like thefe, when Union was the parole of the day, he moft cordially wifhed to fee it in that Court, their thoughts turned to the improvement of their affairs, and their whole undivided ftrength referved for combating the common enemy by " a long pull, a ftrong pull, and a pull altogether," and not exhaufted in the difcuffion of perfonal queflions amongft themfelves. Here then, for the prefent, he would leave the perfonal queflion, in hope that fome honourable friends near him would endeavour to adopt fome mo- dification that fhall embrace the meaning of the whole Court, while he fhould endeavour to fhew, as a means of ftrongly influencing fuch a difpofition, that as there had been no crime there could be no criminal ; and that, inftead of contending whether any particular name fhould or fhould not be included in a Bill of Difcovery, that all fuch Bills, and profecutions of every defcription, ought to ceafe *inftanter*. And the ground he took for this was, that this trade, called *illicit*, is not illicit, becaufe, though irregular, it has been connived at and tole- rated almoft ever fince the birth of the Eaft-India Company ; and, confequently, whatever is fo tolerated and fanctioned, by long practice, cannot be *illegal*. Mr. Moore then went into a long difcuffion of the trade called neutral, contra- band, and illicit, and proved, by a great variety of inftances and authorities, that this trade, however irregular, was neither contraband or illicit, and that the terms themfelves were very little underftood; that the whole of this trade ought, and he hoped foon would, be brought into the River Thames under regular

licence,

licence, and a *Grand Entrepoſt* formed which would render the whole Conti-
nent of Europe dependent on us ; and, as the Miniſter, Mr. Dundas, had very
properly ſaid in the Houſe of Commons (part of whoſe ſpeech Mr. Moore here
read and argued in ſupport of), muſt ſecure to this country thoſe advantages
which our undiſputed pre-eminence in India gave us, and that tribute which, on
being exported, it muſt draw from the other nations of Europe—

Mr. *Henchman* called Mr. Peter Moore to order. He ſaid, he aſked the
honourable Gentleman's pardon for interrupting him, but he believed he was
not upon a topic immediately before the Court. The preſent queſtion was,
whether Mr. Scott was guilty or not guilty of the charges laid againſt him,
whereas the honourable gentleman was entering very largely into the general
trade of India. Mr. Henchman ſaid, he was ſenſible of the value of what fell
from the honourable Proprietor, and at a proper time he would ſolicit the information he was able to give, but he ſubmitted, whether at preſent it was not
rather irrelevant to the queſtion, and therefore he hoped the honourable Proprietor would defer what he had to ſay until the bill relative to the ſhipping
came forward, when the trade of India at large muſt alſo be diſcuſſed. Mr.
Henchman ſaid, he begged to appeal to the Chair, he might be miſtaken in
his opinion, and a point of order was of courſe matter to be decided on by
the honourable Baronet to whom he had the honour to addreſs himſelf.

The CHAIRMAN expreſſed himſelf to be averſe to interrupt any Gentleman,
and by calling to order preventing him from giving his opinion in his own way,
but he ſaid, being appealed to for his opinion, he muſt declare it to be that the
honourable Proprietor (Mr. Moore) was out of order, and more eſpecially ſo,
after the notice that had been given of an intention to bring forward, on an
early day, the very queſtion which the honourable Proprietor now endeavoured
irrelevantly to diſcuſs.

Mr. *Moore* replied, he certainly was in the diſpoſal of the Court, and profeſſed himſelf one of the laſt in it who would intentionally treſpaſs on its
time : but, he did conceive and contend, that he was perfectly in order under
the ſpecial call of the Court to conſider further the papers printed on the ſubject of Illicit Trade, of which the motion before the Court was only a part, and

L   that

that if fuch a difcuffion was to be precluded by the notice of any Proprietor to enter on it at a future day, after the Court was fpecially affembled for its inflant confideration, it was tantamount to a motion of adjournment carried by an individual voice only, and as this was a doctrine to which he could not fub-fcribe, he muft contend for the right of proceeding to the general difcuffion of the papers before them.—[Several Proprietors here applying to Mr. Moore and requefling him to give way, he faid, fince it feemed to be the wifh of the Court he moft certainly would, but the right he maintained.]

Mr. *Huddleftone* faid, he had not read the Papers, but the hon. Proprietor's mó-tion comprehended two things not neceffarily connected with each other ; if he would leave out the former part of the motion he would readily agree to the lat-ter. The hon. Director had already confented to have his name included in the Bill of Difcovery, therefore he faw no neceffity for the former part of the mo-tion. He was ready to acknowledge, that the late Chairman had adopted a hafty refolution, which he had no doubt was at this moment a fubject of regret to him. He appears to have formed conclufions upon circumftances which were too flight to warrant them. He wifhed he had purfued a more moderate line of conduct. He recommended it to the Court to endeavour to conciliate the parties. He felt himfelf placed in an aukward fituation which made it difficult to acquit one without condemning the other.

Mr. *William Lufhington* faid, that the honourable Proprietor had not under-ftood the firft part of the motion. After the Court of Proprietors had declared that there was no neceffity for including the name of the Honourable Director in a Bill of Difcovery, and the Court of Directors had, merely in compliance with the wifh of the honourable Director, departed from the refolution of the General Court, the firft part of the refolution became neceffary in order to ex · plain the ground of the deviation.

Mr. *Auriol* faid, it appeared to him that the whole Court were unanimous in their opinion that Mr. Scott was perfectly innocent of the charges brought againft him, he fhould therefore recommend that his name might be left out of the Bill.

Mr.

Mr. *Henchman* faid, he apprehended it was not the intention of the Directors to file a bill againft Mr. Scott unlefs they fhould fee grounds of fufpicion. The honourable Director had allowed his name to be inferted in the draft of the bill which had been tranfmitted to the Attorney General in order for him to decide whether the profecution fhould be carried on ? In doing this the Directors had gone a ftep beyond what they fhould have done. It now refted upon the judgment of the Attorney General to acquiefce in the ftep which the Directors had taken. It was gone beyond their power to recall.

Mr. *Auriol* expreffed himfelf perfectly fatisfied with the explanation given, and hoped that the fentiments of the Court that day upon the conduct of Mr. Scott, would induce the Attorney General not to agree to the refolution of the Directors.

Mr. *Chifholme* faid, that the honourable Proprietor over the way who had objected to his motion, had prefaced it by faying, that he had not read the papers ; however he might refpect him individually, after fuch a declaration he could not pay much deference to his opinion on this fubject. In wording his motion Mr. Chifholme faid, he had been purpofely concife, and faid no more than was effential to the acquittal of Mr. Scott.

Mr. *Impey* faid, he could not refrain from making an obfervation on a circumftance of fimilarity between this and another celebrated accufation, which he thought highly honourable to the parties accufed ; he was prefent in Weftminfter Hall with great fatisfaction at the acquittal of a late Governor General of Bengal ; at that period the charges were divided into two parts fuch as were fupported by evidence, and fuch as were entirely unfupported. The queftion being firft put upon the former, we all know the defendant was honourably acquitted, when the Court proceeded to put the queftion on the latter ; one Peer and one only pronounced him guilty of thofe charges which were unfupported by any evidence at all. In this laft circumftance, the cafe of the honourable Director exactly refembles it ; we unanimoufly acquit him of having betrayed the fecret of the Manilla expedition, and of being concerned in the Helfingoer, charges on which there is evidence brought forward, fuch as

it

it is ; but as to his being concerned in the illicit commerce to Batavia, of which there is no evidence at all, one Proprietor and one only has thought fit to impute it to him.

Mr. *Robert Thornton* faid, he felt the delicate fituation in which the Court was placed, and he never felt himfelf in a more delicate predicament than at this moment. He had but one obfervation to make, but he found the impulfe to ftate it irrefiftable. He fhould only fpeak to one point, he would allude to no other part of the debate. Having lately been in the direction and knowing how extremely unpleafant it was to witnefs the altercations which the fubject now before the Court had given rife to, he could not help exprefling a hope that the vote of that day would put an extinguifher on all the animofities which had grown out of the fubject, and that the embers of animofity after being fmothered in that Court would not be rekindled in the other room. He hoped here the altercation would be finally fettled, and that if it fhould be determined that the profecution was to go on, that no ftrong language would be ufed on the occafion. He confidered the characters of both the honourable Gentlemen to be immaculate, and he hoped the friends of both would enjoy the fatisfaction of feeing them reconciled to each other.

The CHAIRMAN then put the queftion which was carried *unanimoufly*.

Mr. *David Scott* rofe to fay, that notwithftanding the feelings of innocence with which he had entered the Court, he could not avoid exprefling the heartfelt fatisfaction which their very honourable acquittal had given him, and on which he fhould reflect with the higheft gratification to the laft hour of his life.

Mr. *Baber* moved the queftion of adjournment, which being feconded,

Mr. *Twining* faid, he was not a little furprized at a motion for adjournment immediately following the difcuffion which had taken place, after he had, in the courfe of delivering his opinion on the printed Papers, exprefsly given notice of his intention, when the motion before the Court had been difpofed of, to move a Refolution, fimilar to that which had paffed the Court of Directors, of

thanks

thanks to the late Chairman, and conveying the fentiments of the Court of the purity of the motives upon which he had proceeded. He could not help thinking, that there was great want of candour in thus interpofing the queftion of adjournment, and thereby precluding him from going into the grounds upon which he meant to fupport the refolution he had alluded to. He hoped, after what he ftated, that the honourable Proprietor, who had brought forward the motion, would be induced to withdraw it. If, however, it was the fenfe of the Court to perfift in it, he muft fubmit to their decifion.

Mr. *Henchman* faid, he hoped his honourable friend would not withdraw his motion, but perfevere in it. He did not fee how he could be accufed of want of candour in fuch a propofition. The honourable Proprietor, who wifhed to confirm the vote of thanks to Mr. Bofanquet, could if he thought it expedient fet forth all he had to offer on that fubject as reafons againft the motion of adjournment, therefore he was not precluded from faying all he wifhed to fay. But, Mr. Henchman faid, he really thought it the moft conciliating and therefore the beft plan to end the debate by a fhort queftion, inftead of going into arguments that could not be kept clear of perfonality, and would only tend to difturb the peace of the Court. He therefore fhould fupport the motion of adjournment, and he hoped Gentlemen on the other fide would fee that it was difcreet to allow the bufinefs of the day to come to a conclufion by the means propofed, which could give offence to no man.

Mr. *Durant* faid, he wifhed the queftion for adjournment had not been fo haftily put, for he meant to have afked feveral queftions which were very important. He did not like that the Court fhould be taken by furprize in that manner.

Mr. *Henchman* obferved to the honourable Proprietor, that he was not precluded by the motion that had been made from afking any queftions he might think proper, which, when propofed, would be in order, as he would ftate the afking them as reafons operating with him either to induce him to vote for or againft the motion of adjournment.

M

The

The CHAIRMAN faid, that a motion for adjournment having been moved and feconded, it was irregular to afk any queftions of the Chair until the motion was difpofed of.

Mr. *Kemble* faid, it was illiberal to take the opportunity of moving for an adjournment inftantly after the firft motion was difpofed of, when an honourable Proprietor had previoufly given notice of his intention to follow it up by another. It was but fair, and he hoped the Court would think fo, to hear what the honourable Proprietor had to fay in fupport of his motion of thanks, and if it was not withdrawn by the honourable mover of it for that purpofe, to put a negative upon it.

Mr. *William Lufhington* faid, that if the motion for an adjournment had not been made, and the honourable Proprietor had preffed upon the Court his Refolution of Thanks 'to the late Chairman, he fhould have endeavoured to have got rid of it by moving the previous queftion. He would fairly ftate to the Court his motive for doing fo. It was that notwithftanding the general impreffion he had in favour of the late Chairman as a man of ability and integrity, he could not approve of his conduct, nor help thinking that he had, by bringing forward the charges in the manner he had done, acted intemperately and rafhly. But though with this impreffion he could not approve, neither could he by any exprefs refolution pointedly condemn, his conduct. He could not concur in any motion for thanks, nor would he join in any vote of cenfure. He hoped his honourable Friend, whofe prudence he was well acquainted with, would fee, after this hint, in what a difagreeable predicament the Court would be placed if he perfifted in his intention, and trufted that he would fuffer the matter to remain as it now ftood.

The queftion of adjournment was then put and carried.

www.ingramcontent.com/pod-product-compliance
Lightning Source LLC
Chambersburg PA
CBHW021559270326
41931CB00009B/1300